Welcome to Medo's Hugs!

We hope you are entertained and spend many hours practicing your sketching and coloring skills.

Thc author left you some creative freedom so you can decide whether Medo would look cuter if his fur was orange, pink or even blue! You can make him look fuzzy or even draw his fur all curly and wild.

Follow our (not so) little hero: @MedoMCcat

More books about Medo and his animal friends are coming soon.

When the sun is out,
Medo likes to sit in the soft grass.
It tickles his paws
and smells fresh and sweet.

Sometimes, a little
butterfly dances by...
and Medo just watches,
thoughtful and still,
because he would
not hurt a fly...
or a butterfly!

Medo's favorite pastime is taking naps in the grass. As he sleeps, sparrows play in his lush, soft fur.

Dado loves
to give Medo
BIG, SQUEEZY
hugs!

Medo is not
a fan of being
smothered with
love!

But when Tanya hugs him,
Medo purrs and melts

Her hugs are soft cozy,
just the way Medo likes.

No matter how big the squeeze,
or how silly the hugs,
Medo knows one thing for sure:
He is very, very loved.

Made in the USA
Columbia, SC
06 June 2025